Stamping

Lindsay Mason

ISBN Number: 978-1-907267-03-1

First published in Great Britain 2009

masterCRAFT
Magmaker Ltd
Cromwell Court, New Road,
St Ives, Cambs PE27 5BF, UK

ISBN Number: 978-1-907267-03-1

The Publishers and author can accept no responsibility for any consequences arising from the information, advice or instructions given in this publication.

Readers are permitted to reproduce any of the items in this book for their personal use, or for the purposes of selling for charity, free of charge and without the prior permission of the Publishers. Any duplicated use of the items for commercial purposes is strictly not permitted.

Published by:	Magmaker Ltd, Cromwell Court,
	New Road, St Ives, Cambs PE27 5BF, UK
	t: 01480 496130
	f: 01480 495514
	w: www.magmaker.co.uk
Author:	Lindsay Mason
Editor:	Peter Law
	e: peter.law@magmaker.co.uk
Design:	Lucy Kirkman, RMG Design + Print Ltd
	w: www.rmgpublishing.co.uk
Photography:	Brett Caines
Publishing director:	Peter Raven

Stocked by most good craft shops or available at £4.95 plus p&p
from e: mastercraft@magmaker.co.uk

Contents

Introduction

Stamping dates back many centuries, when images carved into wooden blocks were used to decorate fabrics and papers in China and East Asia.

Many materials have been used through the years to produce repeat designs on various surfaces. Most of us can remember cutting simple patterns into halved potatoes and using these to print bold colours.

In the late 19th Century rubber stamps began to be manufactured and used, mainly for marking products and, later, by banks and libraries. This was mainly thanks to Charles Goodyear, who discovered that the secret to stabilising rubber was to heat it to a high temperature. It was in the 1970s that rubber stamps began to be made and used for recreational use on a grand scale, and led on to the phenomenon that it has become today. Both unmounted rubber and clear acrylic stamps are also now widely available.

There are many reasons why stamping has such a wide appeal. Those who regard themselves as not being artistic are able to be creative with images that they can colour and use in their own way. A stamp is a one-off investment which can be used over and over again, lasting for many years, and the versatility of stamps means that each one can be used in many different ways. From a simply inked and coloured stamp, to elaborate designs featuring embossing, decoupage, distressing and everything in between, there's something for everyone in this addictive craft.

Although the main focus of stamping is obviously the stamps themselves, there are many related products which add to the variety of what can be created. There are countless inks, powders and paints, for instance, all of which will give different effects and can turn a simple stamped design into a work of art.

If you're new to stamping then I hope that this book will help you to find your way through what can seem an overwhelming subject to begin with. If you already enjoy stamping then I hope that you'll find inspiration to try a new technique or style.

Lindsay Mason

Materials & equipment

There are a myriad of inkpads, embossing powders and stamps available now and, if you're just embarking on this addictive craft, it can be rather daunting. As you progress you'll probably want to add to your kit, but, to begin with, there are some basic things that are essential to stamping.

STAMPS

These come in three basic types, all of which will produce great results. Which you prefer to use is a matter of taste..

Wooden backed are the original, and, some would say, best, types of stamp. They should be cleaned with a dedicated stamp cleaner or alcohol-free baby wipes. They provide a firm grip to ensure a clear image and usually have a coloured image on the top which can be helpful as a guide to anyone who is not confident about colouring.

Unmounted rubber stamps come without the wood backing. You'll need to use them with acrylic blocks to provide a stable hand grip when stamping with them. They work best if mounted onto a special foam, such as EZ Mount, which has a cushioning effect and a surface that clings to the acrylic blocks without the need for adhesive.

Clear stamps are transparent. They cling straight onto an acrylic block. The advantage of this type of stamp is that you can see exactly where your image will be, so they are very useful when aligning images.

INKPADS

There are many types of inkpad available, but they fall, basically, into three distinct categories:

Pigment inkpads usually have a slow-drying ink that is especially designed for using with embossing powder. Nowadays, there are lots of pigment inks which will dry without being embossed, whilst some have a chalky finish and others give a watermark effect. If you're in doubt, read the user guidelines on the back of the inkpad.

Dye-based inkpads can be regarded as the basic type for 'flat' stamping. The ink is water-based and dries quickly without heating. Countless colours are available and they can be used directly onto a stamp, or the ink can be picked up with a paintbrush to colour an image.

Wooden backed are the most versatile type of stamps as they can be used in many techniques.

Permanent inkpads are extremely useful as you're able to colour an image immediately without any risk of the ink smudging. They can be used on acetate and glass and, once dry, will be permanent. A special cleaner must be used to remove the ink from your stamps as some are solvent-based.

EMBOSSING POWDERS

These are thermographic powders which melt when heat is applied using a heat gun. They come in a range of colours from clear through to black and special effects such as holographic.

The powder is shaken over an image, stamped using pigment ink, and then a heat gun is directed at the powder until it melts. Care should be taken not to overheat the powder or it will sink back into the card, so it's worth practising on spare card until you get a feel for how much heat to apply. It's also best to start with metallic powders, as it is very obvious once these have melted.

The resulting image will be raised and therefore very easy to colour in, with defined 'walls'. UTEE (Ultra Thick Embossing Enamel) is a much more granular powder and is used for 'triple embossing' to create a very glossy, thick surface which can be stamped into.

So here's a list of materials which will be useful in most, if not all, the projects featured:

- Wooden backed stamps
- Clear stamps (If using these, you'll need an acrylic block to stick them to)
- Unmounted rubber stamps (If using these, you'll need to back them with E-Z mount to allow you to stick them to an acrylic block)
- Inkpads: pigment, dye-based and permanent
- Embossing powders in various colours
- Heat tool
- Colouring mediums - brush pens, pencil crayons, chalks, gel pens etc
- Card stock in various colours including white
- Card blanks
- Guillotine or trimmer
- Scissors
- Craft knife and cutting mat
- Glossy Accents - for adding clear highlights and as a strong adhesive
- Double-sided tape
- Glue pen
- 3D foam tape or squares
- Silicone glue
- Blending foam or sponge pieces
- Waterbrush or paintbrush and water
- Non-stick craft sheet or baking sheet

HEAT GUNS

If you wish to use embossing powders then you'll need a dedicated heat gun - a hairdryer will not work, as it is not hot enough and also blows too fast.

There are various brands available and although they all do a similar job, it is worth noting the difference in order to make an educated choice when buying one.

The hairdryer-shaped guns tend to be quieter and use a more gentle heat. This is very useful when working with shrink plastic, for instance, as the plastic is more easily controlled, whilst the quieter motor may appeal to those wishing to craft at unsociable hours! The more tubular-shaped guns are often much louder and have a fiercer heat which makes them faster and especially useful if you are working with UTEE.

With any of the heat tools it's important to hold them at a 45 degree angle and about 8cm away from the cardstock, moving the tool slowly and steadily across the surface as the powder melts. Do not hold the gun perpendicular to the surface as this may overheat the nozzle and some models will cut out for a few minutes.

Other things you'll need

You'll need an assortment of pens and pencils to colour your stamped images. Gel pens are easy to use and brush pens can be used directly or with a paintbrush to lighten the colours. Watercolour pencils can also be used in this way.

Cardstock is essential and, for general stamping, a bright white card of 160gsm is perfect.

A trimmer or guillotine will be needed for cutting the cardstock accurately, and you may wish to use a craft knife and cutting mat for cutting curved shapes. Good scissors are also essential.

A non-stick craft sheet is extremely useful for protecting your work surface and is also an ideal surface for some inking techniques.

You'll need an assortment of adhesives: double-sided tape, silicone glue, 3D foam squares, and a glue pen will all be useful for different jobs.

There are lots of other materials which you may wish to add to your collection, such as decorating chalks, Mica powders, glazes etc, and these will be covered within the project pages where appropriate.

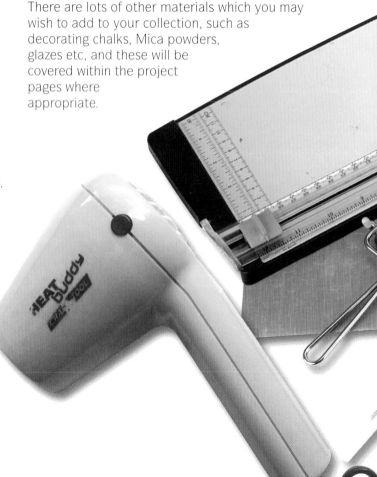

Preparation

A little organisation beforehand will help you to work cleanly and efficiently. Prepare your worktop by ensuring that it is free from any build-up of glue etc which might create an unstable surface for stamping onto.

If you don't have a stamp mat, place a few sheets of paper on your table to provide some cushioning – this will help to give a clearer impression, particularly when working with clear stamps on acrylic blocks.

Keep the heat tool switched off at the mains, or unplugged, until you're ready to use it, as this will avoid switching it on accidentally. Be careful to keep the electric lead safely away from your gullotine, trimmer or scissors.

Greasy or inky fingers will leave unwanted marks on your work and may also attract embossing powder in areas where it was not intended to stick! Clean your hands regularly and try sweeping an anti static pad across cardstock before stamping onto it. Tumble dryer sheets, or a cotton sock with a little talc inside it, can also be used for this purpose.

Look after your stamping equipment and it will last you for many years. Clean rubber stamps by using a dedicated stamp cleaner and dry on a wadge of kitchen paper or a scrubby mat. They can also be cleaned with alcohol-free baby wipes. Acrylic stamps are the only ones that can be washed under the tap. To clean very grubby stamps, use washing-up liquid on an old toothbrush and give them a good scrub before drying on paper towel. Permanent inks, such as Stazon, must be cleaned off stamps using a solvent-based stamp cleaner.

Store wooden stamps either on their sides, or rubber side down on a flat surface. If you need to stack them, try not to have more than two layers to avoid too much weight pressing on them. Store the biggest stamps on the bottom layer.

Inkpads should always have their lids replaced as quickly as possible and be stored flat with the lids uppermost. Re-inkers are available for most inkpads as they become less juicy.

Basic techniques

Step by Step Instructions

The most basic technique is to stamp an image and colour it in. Different effects can be achieved by varying the colouring medium. Coloured pencils or chalks will give a soft, powdery finish, ideal for shading images of animals or anything textural. Brush pens can be used neat, or with water and a brush, to give a painted appearance where shading is needed, such as on flowers or faces. Gel pens, which may have a shimmery or glitter effect, are particularly fun to use with bold or cute stamps.

When inking a stamp, place the stamp face up on your worksurface and tap the inkpad lightly over it. This prevents you applying too much ink, which might give a 'halo' effect around the image. Check that the surface looks well inked before pressing firmly down onto card and lifting cleanly away. Large stamps should be pressed all over with the knuckles of one hand, whilst keeping the stamp held firmly in place with the other. Never take both hands off the stamp or it may smudge. To ink a very small stamp, you may wish to hold it in one hand and tap the ink onto it so that you can control where the ink is going.

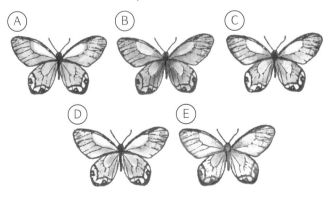

Image A   Brush pens used neat.
Image B   Brush pens watered down and painted on.
Image C   Crayons used neat.
Image D   Chalks.
Image E   Glitter gel pens.

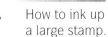

Image A   How to ink up a large stamp.

Image B   How to press a stamp down.

Image C   How to ink up a small stamp.

continued

Heat embossing will turn the flat lines on an image into raised ones, usually with a metallic effect. Colouring an embossed image is quite easy, as the raised lines form a 'wall' to stop colours crossing into the wrong areas. Choose bold images to emboss, as very detailed ones will tend to look blurry as shown here. Detail embossing powder is finer than the standard type, but should still be avoided on very fine images.

A heat gun must be used with embossing powders and it should always be held a few inches above the image at an angle of about 45 degrees. This not only avoids overheating, but the residual heat moving across the card will also speed up the process. To allow the heat to pass through, and to protect your hands and worksurface, it's a good idea to place the stamped images onto another piece of card and hold this in the air whilst heating.

Image stamped
and not embossed.

Image embossed
with Detail black
embossing powder.

Image embossed
with normal gold
embossing powder.

Using a heat tool at the correct angle and height.

Trouble shooting

Problem: When I stamp I get a halo effect of ink around the image.
Answer: You're applying too much ink. Be sure to take the inkpad to the stamp, not the other way round. Tap the ink lightly onto the stamp and don't 'squidge' it down onto the rubber. Check the rubber after inking up and, if you can see any excess ink on the edges, simply wipe it away with your thumb, or a cotton bud, before stamping.

Problem: When I emboss I get specks of powder all over the background card.
Answer: Any grease or ink on your fingers will transfer to the card and may attract stray embossing powder. To avoid this, keep your hands clean and dry – baby wipes are a handy addition to your work table. Sweep an anti-static pad across the card before stamping which will also help to repel stray granules. If you still have problems, avoid coloured embossing powders and use a clear one that can be applied over any colour of pigment ink – any specks of this will be less apparent.

Problem: When I emboss an image it doesn't look raised and metallic. Instead it looks flat and greasy.
Answer: This is a common problem for newcomer stampers and is caused by overheating. Make sure that you hold the heat tool at a 45 degree angle and move it slowly across the image. Once you can see the embossing powder changing its appearance move on to another area. If you keep heating it, it will sink back into the card and leave a greasy looking outline. Use gold powder to begin with, as this alters dramatically, making it easier to know when it has been sufficiently heated.

Problem: My stamped image looked perfect, but when I began colouring it, the outline bled and ruined the colours.
Answer: This is due to the type of ink you used on the stamp, or by applying colours too soon after stamping.

Using a permanent ink, such as Stazon, Archival, or Memories, will allow you to colour in immediately. If you're using a non-permanent ink, such as a dye-based, heat the image to set the ink. If you're unsure, ask your retailer to recommend a fast-drying inkpad. You can also use coloured pencils or chalks to avoid smudging, as these are a dry pigment.

Problem: I have tried colouring directly onto a stamp with pens, but the image was pale and very patchy.
Answer: The ink from pens dries very quickly, so you need to re-activate it before pressing the stamp down. To do this, simply breathe over the coloured surface of the stamp which is known as 'huffing'. You may also wish to try spritzing water over the coloured stamp for a watercoloured effect. Be sure to set the image straight away with a heat tool when using this method.

Problem: I want to use pens to colour my images, but I find I get hard lines that don't blend well.
Answer: Try using a waterbrush to soften the pigment. Scribble the pen onto an acrylic block, or non-stick surface, then pick up some colour with a brush and paint the image. This method allows you to shade the colours easily by adding less, or more, water and shades can be blended into each other. Alternatively, you may wish to invest in a blender pen, which softens harsh edges.

Problem: I'm just hopeless at colouring in, but I don't want everything I stamp to stay black and white.
Answer: Try using the technique of painting with paper. By stamping several times onto different coloured and patterned papers, cutting sections out from each image and layering them back up, you can create a coloured image without having to use pens or crayons. Also, try inking the stamp using a rainbow pad, which will create an array of colour across the image.

Decoupaging your stamps

Rubber stamps are a great tool for creating your own three-dimensional images and, unlike the traditional decoupage sheets, can be used time and again as much as you wish.

Some stamps have greater potential for decoupaging than others, so do choose images carefully. A flower bouquet, for instance, may seem an ideal candidate, but check that there are not too many very fiddly areas that would be tricky to cut out. The image should also be one with some perspective, ie: it should have areas that look further back than others, as in the group of flowers used here.

Decoupaging with stamps also gives you the opportunity to colour the image in any colours you choose and in whatever medium you prefer, be it coloured pencils, brush pens or gel pens, for instance.

Start by stamping one image onto white card and cut this out as a panel. You will not need to colour this image in its entirety as much of it will be covered by subsequent layers.

However, rather than just colouring the edges, it is well worth continuing further into the image so that no white areas can be seen if the card is looked at from the side. Work out how many layers you wish to add and then decide which areas will be furthest forward, as you will need to colour more of these.

You can use 3D foam to stick the layers down: these are now available in various depths, sizes and also in white, black or even clear, so you can choose the most appropriate type for your project. The foam squares can be cut down if you need to add support to very small areas. Silicone glue is an excellent alternative as, not only does it allow you to maneouvre a layer to get it correctly positioned, but it also allows you to adjust the height of the layers by applying more, or less, pressure. I have used silicone glue in this project.

You will need:

- Stamp: Floral Arrangement P1501P by Personal Impressions
- Black dye-based or permanent inkpad
- Marvy Le Plume pens in various shades of lilacs, yellows and green
- Waterbrush
- White 160gsm cardstock
- Card stock in lemon and lilac
- White card blank 13cm x 18cm
- Craft knife
- Fine-tipped scissors
- Silicone glue
- Lilac ribbon – approx $^3/_4$ metre
- White paper for insert

For a more finished look it's a good idea to shape the layers before sticking them into position. You can curve the cut-out image around your finger, or use a scissor blade to curve things such as petals or leaves. To give a sheen to the finished piece, coat with decoupage varnish, remembering to check first whether the colours you have used will run. Glossy Accents, or iridescent glitter glue, can be used to add highlights to the centres of flowers etc.

Step by Step Instructions

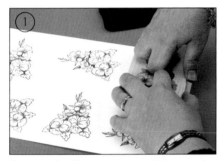

1. Stamp the flowers onto white card six times using a black dye-based or permanent inkpad. Cut one image out as a 9cm x 12cm panel.

2. Colour the edges using brush pens and a waterbrush, remembering to bring the colour some way into the image.

3. Mat the panel onto lemon, lilac and then lemon card again, trimming a narrow border on each panel. Stick the complete panel onto a 13cm x 18cm white card, positioning it nearer to the top.

4. Following the colours on the first one, colour a second entire image, again colouring a little way in from the edges. Carefully cut this out and set aside.

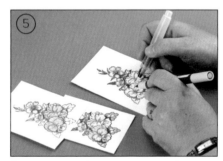

5. Colour a third image, except for the leaves, and, this time, colouring fully. Remember to start with light shades and add darker tones to give realism. Cut out, omitting the leaves.

6. Colour three more sets of the pansies and two more of the primroses.

Cut out one set of pansies, then just the left pansy and then two sets of the small pansy petals.

Cut out both primroses fully and then trim the left petal away from one of the lower ones.

Curl each element slightly using your fingers or scissor blade and set them out in order.

Use a cocktail stick to add blobs of silicone to the base image on the card and carefully lower the largest cut out onto it.

Add silicone to the back of the image with no leaves and place this on top of the second, pressing lightly to avoid flattening those underneath.

Continue to layer up the images from largest to smallest, adding more silicone for an area to stand higher. Allow silicone to set completely

Cut a small slit near the bottom of the card spine and thread a piece of lilac ribbon through, wrapping it around and sticking down the ends inside the card.

Tie a small bow from another piece of the ribbon and stick to the centre of the ribbon with more silicone glue. Stick an insert in the card to cover the ribbon.

Hints & Tips When you're positioning the layers it's a good idea to stand up and look down at the card vertically to ensure accurate placement.

You may wish to run a black pen around the edges of each cut-out image as this will disguise any white areas which may show if you have not cut accurately.

21

Stamping into friendly plastic

Friendly plastic has been around for many years and was used mainly in making jewellery, but it has had something of a revival in popularity since it became known that it could be used in conjunction with rubber stamps. It's sold in bookmark-sized strips in an array of colours, both plain and patterned, metallic, pearlised and opaque.

It can be cut quite easily with scissors and, once heated, it becomes soft and pliable. The plastic will also stick to itself when heated so that various colours can be patched together, or a larger piece can be made from smaller ones. Heating can be done in hot water, the oven or with a heat tool, which is the method used when stamping.

It's vital to work on a non-stick craft sheet or the back of the plastic will adhere to your work surface and become a mess! A Teflon baking sheet can also be used. It's also worth practising on a scrap or two of the plastic to get the feel for how warm it needs to be before stamping into. You'll notice that the surface starts to develop a slight texture which is an indication that it is pliable. Once stamped it's vital to allow the plastic to cool down before lifting the stamp away; if you try to do so too quickly it will stick.

Make sure that the ink that you use on the stamp is one that will dry on the friendly plastic. Permanent inkpads, or those which state that they set on glossy card, will be fine, though some may take a while to become fully dry. The Brilliance ink used in this project is perfect as, although it doesn't dry immediately, it sets with a lovely pearlescent finish. If you're not sure as to the suitability of an inkpad, always ask in the craft shop, or do a test on a small offcut of the plastic first.

You will need:

- Friendly plastic strip in Metallic Pink
- Stamp: 3D Grand Two P1632Q by Personal Impressions
- Brilliance inkpad in Starlight Silver
- Large flat backed gem stone in Aurora Borealis
- Black and silver card stock
- Decorative pink paper
- Non-stick craft or baking sheets
- 15cm square white card blank

Step by Step Instructions

Cut two 8cm lengths of the friendly plastic and keep remaining piece to one side. Gently heat the long edge of one piece and then place the second piece next to it, holding it in position until it adheres.

Place the piece onto the non-stick sheet coloured side up and ink up the stamp with the Brilliance inkpad.

Use the heat tool to warm the plastic, looking for the change in surface texture.

Press the stamp firmly onto the plastic and leave in position to cool down. Once cooled, carefully remove the stamp.

Repeat steps 3 - 4 with the small piece of plastic remaining, ensuring that you stamp the centre of the medallion.

Cut around the full medallion with strong scissors.

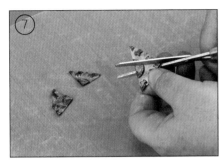

Cut the small piece into a square with the circle in the centre. Now cut the square diagonally into quarters to give four small triangles.

Cut a 9cm square and a 13cm square of black card, a 9.5cm square of silver and a 12cm square of decorative pink paper. Layer these up and attach to the card front.

Stick the large medallion to the centre of the card using a good amount of silicone glue.

Stick the triangles at the corners of the largest black layer of card.

Use silicone glue to stick the gemstone to the middle of the medallion – even if the gem is self-adhesive it is best to use silicone on this surface.

Hints & Tips You could make a brooch by adhering a brooch pin to the back of a stamped piece of the friendly plastic and securing it to a card as a gift.

If you need to cool down friendly plastic quickly, drop it into cold water.

scatter seeds of
kindness
everywhere
you go,
scatter acts of
courtesy
watch them
grow and **grow.**
gather buds of
friendship
keep them till
full grown
you will find more
happiness
than you
have ever known

Watercolour stamping with brush pens

This technique is very satisfying as the results give the impression that the images have been hand-painted. The best effects are achieved by using silhouette, or solid image stamps, rather than those which are basically an outline. Rubber stamps will also work better than acrylic or polymer ones for this particular method.

Choose good quality brush pens as these have a better depth of colour than cheaper versions and are a worthwhile investment as they will last for a long time. As the colours will be applied directly to the stamp, always start with the lightest shades, building up to darker hues to avoid contaminating the pens. You don't need to be neat or precise when colouring, as the areas will blend together once they are wetted.

The word stamp is coloured in the same way but, rather than wetting the image, it's breathed on, known as 'huffing'. This remoistens the colours whilst retaining the clarity of the words.

Best results will come from working onto smooth watercolour paper, but any fairly absorbent card stock can be used, and it's worth trying various surfaces to see what different effects these give.

You'll also need a water spritzer and, again, it's worth getting one that gives a fine mist of water rather than the cheaper types which can often sputter and create large blobs of liquid that may spoil your work.

Practise a few times before starting on the actual project to gauge how much water you need to spritz onto the stamp, as it's a common mistake not to get the image wet enough to give a true watercoloured effect. When you first lift the stamp away from the paper the image will look rather messy, but as it's heated the colours will sharpen and become clearer. The heat should be applied as soon as the image has been stamped to give the best effect.

Step by Step Instructions

You will need:

- Floral and sentiment rubber stamps (I used Darkroom Door unmounted rubber set: DDRS017 Friendship Flowers)
- Smooth watercolour paper cut to 16cm square
- 19cm square white card blank
- Card for matting in deep and medium pink
- Brush pens in assorted colours (you'll need three shades of each colour and at least two shades of green)
- Water spritzer
- Soft paint brush
- Heat tool
- Non-stick surface such as an acrylic block
- Double-sided tape

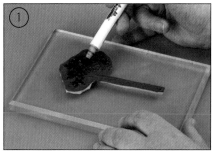

Colour the whole flower head with a pale pink brush pen.

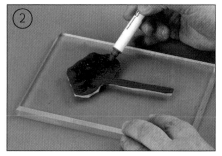

Add a medium pink to random areas of the flower and the dark pink to smaller areas.

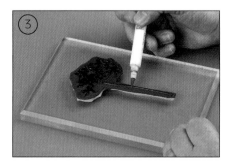

Apply light, and then dark, greens to the flower stems and leaves.

Hold the stamp flat in your hand and spritz it with water.

Hints & Tips It's worth having a scrap piece of the same paper as that which you'll be working on so that you can try out various colour combinations before committing yourself to them on the finished card.

Press the stamp straight down onto a 16cm square of watercolour paper and lift away immediately.

Blast the image with the heat tool until it is completely dry.

Add more flowers in the same way, using various colour combinations.

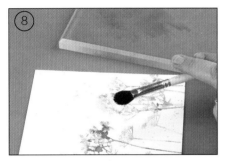

Scribble some colours onto a non-stick surface and add water to thin them down. Pick up the colour with a soft brush and flick lightly above the stamped paper to create a light spattering effect.

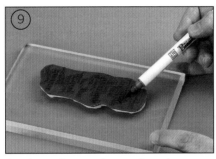

Apply various colours directly to the sentiment stamp and breathe on the image to re-moisten the ink.

Press down firmly at one side of the flower panel and allow to dry.

Mat the panel onto deep, and then medium pink card, leaving narrow borders all round.

Stick the matted image onto a 19cm square white card blank.

Resist technique

Along with embossing, this is probably one of the most 'magical' techniques in rubber stamping. By simply applying dye-based colours over clear, glycerine-based ink, a stamped image will pop out. The effect is dependent upon using a glossy cardstock which, ideally, should be cast coated as this has the optimum surface. Other gloss card will work, but photographic papers will not.

Choose images that are quite bold for maximum impact, remembering that they will show up as a paler version of the surrounding colour. Dedicated Resist inkpads are available, but a Versamark Watermark inkpad will also work just as well if you already have one of these.

The coloured, dye-based inks can be applied with sponge, a foam applicator or a brayer roller as used here. The brayer must be rolled, lifted, and rolled again on the inkpad to fully coat the roller. Remember that if you're using a rainbow, or striped, inkpad, you must roll the brayer only in the direction of the colour bands and not across them, to avoid contamination of the shades.

Begin by stamping an image onto the gloss card with the Resist, or Watermark, ink and then use the heat tool to dry the ink to avoid smudging. Now roll the brayer over the coloured inkpad, lift and roll again to coat it fully before rolling it across the glossy card. The ink will look quite patchy to begin with, but keep rolling in different directions and it will begin to blend. Pick up more colour and roll again, varying the direction as you go. You'll see that the stamped image starts to emerge more as you ink the cardstock.

When you're happy with the effect, allow the ink to dry for a few moments before buffing up the surface with a soft cloth or paper towel. This will remove any excess ink as well as bringing a lovely sheen to the card. You can now cut the card to size for your chosen project.

You will need:

- Rubber stamp: Flower P14935 by Personal Impressions
- Clear stamp set: Build a Flower PICS023 by Personal Impressions
- Brayer roller
- Gloss white card stock
- Resist, or Versamark Watermark inkpad
- Ranger, 'Big and Juicy' Rainbow inkpad - Spice
- Cream card stock
- Hole punch
- Corner rounder punch
- Selection of toning fibres and ribbons
- Adhesive gemstones
- Gold glitter glue

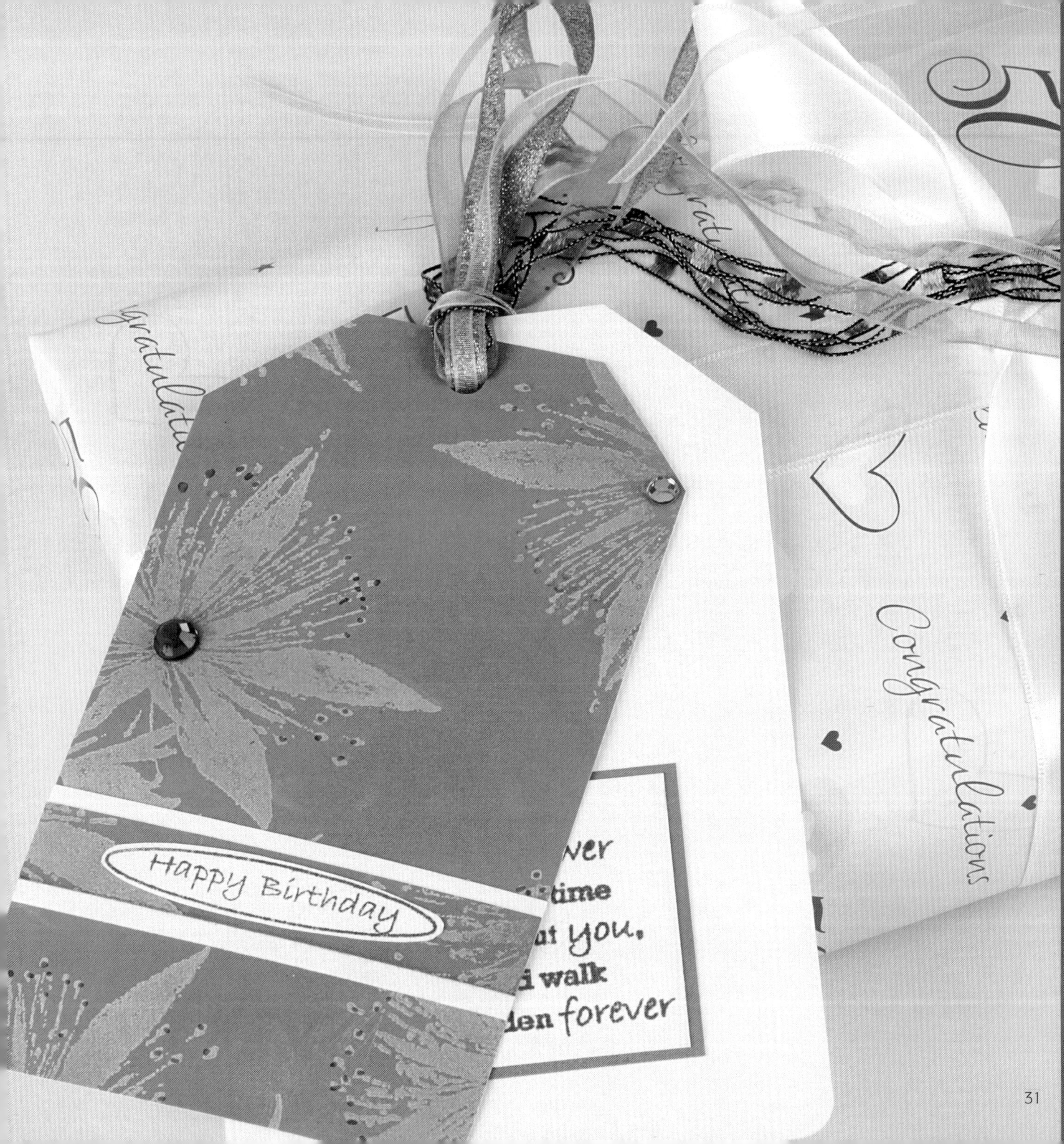

Happy Birthday

...ver
...time
...t you,
...walk
...en forever

Congratulations

Step by Step Instructions

Place a piece of 16cm x 9cm (approximately) gloss white card onto a protected surface. Ink up the stamp with the Watermark pad and apply to the card. Repeat randomly over the card.

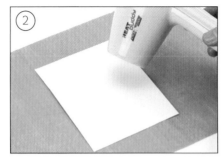

Use the heat tool to dry the stamped images.

Roll the brayer across the rainbow inkpad from front to back. Lift and repeat to coat the roller.

Roll the ink across the card, moving it in different directions to blend the ink.

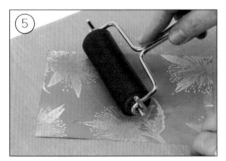

Keep applying ink until the card is covered and the images are revealed.

Once the ink is dry, buff the surface with a soft cloth or paper towel.

Hints & Tips Work on a larger piece of card than your project requires and then trim to size to give a neater finish. Any excess card can then be used to punch shapes from, such as leaves or butterflies.

If your hole punch won't go through both tags together just punch through one, place on top of the second tag and lightly draw round the hole with a pencil. Use this as a guide to punch through the second tag.

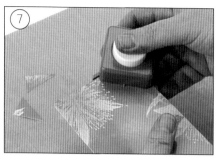

Cut the card to 8cm x 14cm, keeping leftover card for later. Cut two corners to create tag shape and use punch to round two bottom corners.

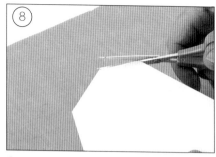

Cut a second tag from cream card, measuring 9cm x 15cm, round the corners and use the stamped tag as a guide for the 'shoulders'. Set aside.

Use the rainbow inkpad to stamp the oval 'Happy Birthday' onto cream card and cut out.

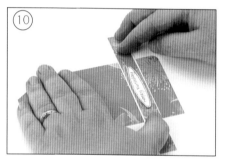

Stick onto the scrap of stamped card and trim to neat strip before matting onto strip of cream. Stick across bottom of stamped tag, trimming ends to fit.

Ink up the sentiment stamp using the rainbow inkpad and stamp onto cream card before cutting out.

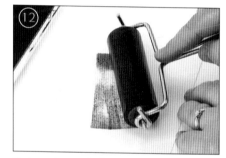

Cut a piece of gloss card to just bigger than the stamped sentiment and brayer the rainbow ink across it. Buff up as before.

Stick the sentiment onto the inked panel and then onto the bottom of the cream tag.

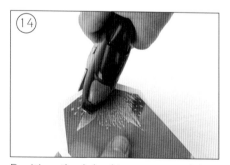

Position the inked tag on top of the cream one and punch a hole at the top through both tags.

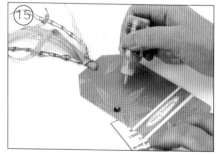

Tie tags together with mix of ribbons and fibres, making sure they're not so tight that tags cannot move. Add self-adhesive gems and dots of gold glitter glue to flower images.

Heat embossing

When crafters embark on rubber stamping, they almost always want to try heat embossing as soon as possible. It isn't surprising, as watching a dull powder turn into a shining metallic finish never fails to appeal.

However, not all stamps are well suited to this technique. Those which are very detailed tend to be far better left simply stamped, as, when embossing powder is heated it melts and slightly spreads. A very detailed image will often be lost, although Detail Powders are available which, having an ultra fine grain, do combat this somewhat. In the main though, bolder, cleaner images will give the best results.

There are a myriad of colours of powder available from clear, through pastel shades, to metallics and black. If you want to emboss an image in black on a pale background it's usually better to use black pigment ink and emboss using clear powder, as this avoids the risk of having stray black specks over the background. As overheating the powder will make it sink back into the card, it's a good idea to practise using metallic powders at first, as these change very dramatically and will give you a feel for how much heat you need to apply.

Whichever powder you use the technique is the same. Stamp an image using a pigment-based inkpad – a clear one will work with any colour of powder. Working over scrap paper, pour a generous amount of powder over the image, tip off the excess and lightly tap the reverse to remove any stubborn specks. If any granules remain, a small, soft brush can be carefully used to flick them away. Begin to heat the powder using an embossing gun, holding it at about a 45 degree angle and working across the image. Do not waggle the heat tool about, but gently move it as the powder melts. Allow it to cool before touching.

In this project the background stamp has been embossed with three different colours by pouring one powder onto certain areas, tipping away, adding a second colour and repeating with a third. Remember to use three sheets of scrap paper to avoid contaminating the powders.

Step by Step Instructions

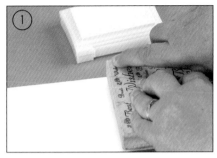

Ink up the background stamp and press it down firmly onto the top section of a 10cm x 20cm strip of white card. Repeat below the first image.

Pour gold embossing powder across the image in three sections. Tip away the excess.

Pour cranberry powder between the gold powder sections. Tip away the excess.

Cover the whole image with Pewter Shimmer powder and tip away the excess. This last powder will fill any gaps.

Heat the powder until you see it change its appearance. Allow to cool, then trim to 8cm wide and mat onto a 9cm wide strip of deep pink card.

Stick the strip down the front of the card blank, slightly to the right, and trim away the excess card.

Hints & Tips If you find that lots of powder is sticking to the background card, try using an anti-static bag (available from craft shops) to sweep across the surface before you stamp the image.

Hints & Tips Try this card with different colour combinations for a completely different look.

Stamp three flowers onto deep pink card and emboss two with gold and one with Pewter Shimmer. Do these one by one to avoid the ink becoming too dry for the powder to cling to.

Use the deep pink brush pen to tint the flower centres and across the embossed detail in the petals. Buff away excess colour with a tissue – the colour will not adhere to the embossed lines.

Cut out each flower and bend the petals up around the centres.

Stick the flowers down the front of the card so that they partially cover the background sentiment.

Lightly touch the Perfect Plumeria inkpad around the edges of the card.

Further examples of embossed images.

Colouring with chalks

For soft and subtle colouring effects, chalks are an ideal medium. A very simple way to make a background layer for a card is to stamp an image randomly using a Versamark Watermark inkpad and then pounce chalk over the ink before gently dusting it away.

Chalks can also be applied directly to a stamped image using a small applicator – these can be similar to eye shadow sponges, pom poms held with an alligator grip tool, or even cotton wool balls. They are easily blended and can also be rubbed away with a chalk eraser. For this project the chalks are applied over a clear ink, which holds the colours in place before varnishing.

Chalks are easily blended by starting with pale shades, adding darker tones and then gently rubbing the colours together with the applicator. Any excess chalk should be simply blown away to avoid leaving fingerprints or smudges.

When using chalks on paper or card there's no need to set them as they're designed to be stable once rubbed into the surface. If you do feel the need to set them, however, you can either use an artist's fixative spray or a very cheap hairspray – the dearer ones contain conditioning oils so don't use these. Simply spray into the air and waft the card underneath rather than spraying directly on. Because this project involves chalking a non-porous surface, the images are coated with a water-based varnish to avoid smudging and also to give a sheen.

Dominoes are an unusual, but very good, surface to work on as they accept ink very readily and are very smooth.

You will need:

- Stamps:
  Quilted Flower Hat P121F
  Fashion Scarf no 1 P1200G
  Fashion Scarf no 2 P1210M
  Broderie Anglaise P1247F
  One Sided Drapery P1263G
  (all from the Beryl Peters collection by Personal Impressions)
- Decorating chalks
- Chalk applicator tools
- Versamark Watermark inkpad
- Black Stazon inkpad
- Metallic gold pen
- Glossy Accents
- Water-based brush on varnish such as Mod Podge
- 1.5cm wide ribbon, approximately 1 metre
- Decorative paper
- Soft wide brush
- Stiff card stock
- Glue dot

Step by Step Instructions

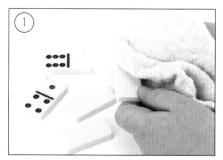

① Wash and dry five dominoes to ensure they are clean.

② Using the Stazon pad, ink up one of the vintage ladies and lay it, inked side upwards, on your work surface.

③ Place a domino down onto the stamp, press firmly and lift cleanly away. Allow to dry.

Hints & Tips If you apply too heavy a colour of chalk, simply dab at it with a clean applicator and this will remove some of the colour.

④ Press the Watermark inkpad all over the stamped side of the domino.

⑤ Pick up some pale pink chalk and gently pounce it over the face and neck before adding a slightly darker shade to the cheeks.

⑥ Continue to add colour to the image, being careful to brush the chalk on gently. Colour the background.

Hints & Tips Children's blackboard chalks will not work as they have very little pigment in them. Artists' chalk pastels can be used, but, as they're designed to be drawn with, they don't release powder when rubbed with a soft applicator and have to be scraped with a blade so that the powder can be used. Dedicated paper-crafting chalks are made especially for the job and are by far the best option – they're readily available in most craft shops.

Use a gold pen to edge the domino and add highlights to the ladies' clothes if you wish.

Use a soft, wide brush to coat the domino with the varnish. Repeat steps 2 - 8 with the remaining four dominoes and set them aside.

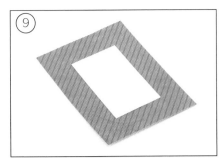

Cut five pieces of card to 3.5cm x 6cm and stick each to the back of decorative paper before cutting 1cm larger all round.

Cut off the corners and fold the sides in, adhering with double-sided tape.

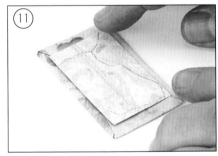

Cut 3cm x 5cm pieces of the paper and stick this over the back to neaten.

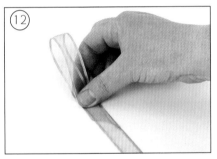

Lay approximately ¾ metre of the ribbon down flat and double one end over by about 12cm.

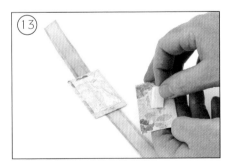

Stick the panels face down onto it using double-sided tape, spacing them with 1cm gaps between.

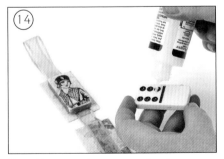

Turn the panels over and using Glossy Accents to stick a domino onto each panel, trap the ribbon between.

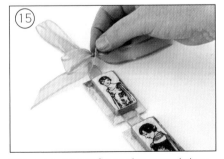

Tie a neat bow from the remaining ribbon and stick above the top panel using a glue dot. Trim the ribbon ends.

Stamping on glass and gilding

For a true touch of luxury, nothing beats the look of gilding! Metal leaf is available in various finishes including gold and silver as well as Abalone and in packs of mixed flake. It's easy to apply and can be used behind acetate as well as glass.

For this project I've used a Memory Glass square and frame to create a sentimental gift. These little frames come in different shapes and sizes and the pieces can be used for jewellery as well as for decorative hangers. If you don't want to buy a ready-made frame, you can use narrow copper foil to bind the edges of the glass and secure a twist of wire to the top, with more foil, as a hanging loop. Use acetate instead of glass if you wish to use the gilded image on the front of a card.

Permanent ink must be used to stamp onto the glass. The best, and safest, way is to place the stamp on its back and lightly press the glass onto the surface. This also allows you to choose which part of the image you're stamping. Remove the glass and allow the ink to set completely. Turn the glass over and place onto white paper so that you can see it clearly, before colouring your chosen areas. This project uses pearlised acrylic paints, as these give a lovely sheen, but you can also use permanent pens if you prefer. Remember that you'll be working from the back, so you cannot add extra colour detail over an already-painted area as it will not show through.

Use the paint with a damp paintbrush to give a creamy texture that is not too thin. The idea is to have solid, rather than transparent, colour. Apply the paint with a dabbing motion rather than brushing it, as this will avoid streaks. Keep turning the glass in your hand so that you can see the effect when viewed from the front. When complete, allow the paint to completely dry naturally; don't be tempted to try to heat set it as the paint may bubble or you may crack the glass.

Use a two-way glue pen to fill in the clear areas of the glass. Two-way glue is usually blue upon application so that you can see where it is, but it dries clear. Once clear, the glue is tacky, and this is when the metal leaf should be applied. If using a sheet of leaf, press it onto the glass, or, if using the mixed flake, drop the glass into the bag and pad the flakes down onto it. Once the leaf is pressed down, use a stiff brush to remove any excess and the piece is now ready to be used in your project.

Step by Step Instructions

- Metal leaf in sheet or flakes
- Stamp: Heart and Nature Collage FP103 by Funstamps
- Black Stazon inkpad
- Pearlised acrylic paints (I used Adirondack)
- Memory glass 5cm square
- Memory glass frame 5cm brass
- Two-way glue pen
- Stiff brush
- Paintbrush – no 2 size is ideal
- Stiff card cut to 5cm square
- Sheer deep red ribbon, approximately 1 metre
- Bone folder or teaspoon
- White paper

① Ink up the stamp with black Stazon and place it face up on your table.

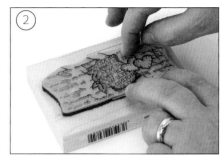

② Place the glass onto the stamp and gently press down with your fingertips.

③ Lift the glass away and allow the ink to set completely.

④ Turn the glass over and place onto white paper.

⑤ Use a damp brush to paint the design with the acrylic paints.

⑥ Keep turning the glass over to check how the paint looks from the front.

Once you're happy with it, set aside to dry completely.

Apply glue pen over the clear areas of the glass, from the back, and allow to become tacky.

Cover the glass with metal leaf and press down.

Brush off the excess leaf with a stiff brush.

Open the little frame and pop the glass panel into it.

Add pre-cut card behind the glass before closing the frame again.

Secure the frame and burnish the fastening clip with a bone folder or teaspoon.

Tie a loop of ribbon through the hanging loop and tie a second piece of ribbon into a bow at the base of the loop.

Hints & Tips Keep metal leaf in a plastic tub with a lid, or a clear bag, and hold the glass in this whilst applying and brushing away the excess. This avoids metal leaf particles covering your worksurface – and carpet!

If you're creating a pendant, you may wish to add a piece of velvet behind the card at the back of the glass for an extra touch of luxury.

All over embossing

This technique makes full use of the effect that is achieved using clear embossing powders which have sparkles in them. The one used here is Hologram, but there are several others such as Stardust and Glitter. Each will give a slightly different finish so it's worth trying them out to see which you prefer, and most craft shops will have samples on show of the various powders so that you can see, in advance, what they look like.

These powders can be used to simply emboss a stamped image, and they look particularly effective against black card. However, when used as a full coverage, the finish is an all-over glitter with no shedding. When you stamp a greeting, or write a name or personalised message, before embossing, the words will be underneath the glitter, giving a very professional finish. It's best to use a medium weight white card to stamp onto, as fully embossing the surface tends to make thin card curl up. It's also worth using double-sided adhesive sheet, as opposed to just using tape, to stick the image down as it will give a stronger adhesion and will ensure that it is completely flat.

It's important to use a fast-drying, or permanent, inkpad to stamp the image so that it can be coloured with brush pens and a waterbrush without any smudging, and also to avoid any transference of ink onto the clear Versamark pad which will be used over the top. If you don't have a waterbrush you can use a brush and a pot of water, although a waterbrush is a good investment as it saves time and negates the possibilities of accidents with spilled water!

The words featured on this project were added using the 'stick and dot' technique, which is a useful addition to any crafter's skills – especially for those of us who don't have particularly attractive handwriting! Do try this simple script as it is especially useful for whimsical projects and allows you to personalise them.

There are no exact measurements given for this project as you may be working with a notebook of a different size to the one which I used. Simply cut the card and matting layers to fit the dimensions of your chosen book.

Step by Step Instructions

You will need:

- Fairy stamp (I used 3017L Iris Fairy from the Flower Fairy collection by Personal Impressions)
- Brush pens
- Black Stazon inkpad
- Versamark Watermark inkpad
- Hologram embossing powder
- Medium weight white card
- Yellow card
- Blue card
- Toning decorative paper
- Assortment of toning ribbons
- Double-sided adhesive sheet
- Double-sided tape
- Spiral bound notebook
- Heat tool
- Trimmer or guillotine

Hints & Tips Try all over embossing onto patterned papers to create a glittered finish which won't shed.

Stamp the fairy image onto medium weight white card which is just smaller than the notebook.

Scribble colours onto a non-stick surface and water down slightly with a brush.

Paint the stamped image beginning with the lightest colour in an area and adding darker tones to shade. Allow to dry.

Add words above fairy by writing bold letters with fine point of the pen and then adding a dot to the end of each line using the thicker end.

Set all the colours using the heat tool.

Cover the whole piece of card using the Versamark Watermark inkpad in a pressing, rather than sweeping, movement.

Immediately cover the card with the Hologram embossing powder.

Shake off excess powder onto paper to tip back into the jar and use heat tool to melt the powder on card, taking care not to overheat.

Stick double-sided adhesive sheet over the back of the card and trim to about 1.5cm smaller than the notebook.

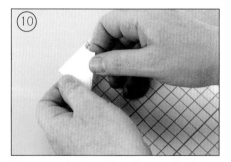

Remove the backing film and stick the image onto yellow card, trimming a narrow border all around.

Use double-sided tape to stick matted image onto blue card, decorative paper and then yellow card, trimming a narrow border round each in turn.

Stick the matted image onto the front of a spiral bound notebook.

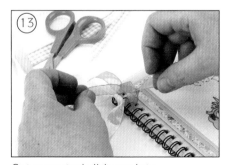

Cut assorted ribbons into approximately 15cm lengths and tie one around each spiral on the notebook.

Trim the ribbon ends into neat points.

Hints & Tips

Make sure that the Versamark Watermark pad that you're using is clean so that you don't transfer any dirty marks onto the white card.

When shading the image, use a more watered-down colour for the main area and use the same colour with less water to add darker tones.

Triple embossing

Although this technique is usually referred to as triple embossing, it can, in fact, comprise more layers than that, depending on the look required. The finished effect is a glass-like enamel. The embossing powder which creates the finish is called Utra Thick Embossing Enamel (or UTEE for short) and is much more granular than general embossing powders. The most commonly used one is clear, although metallic and vivid colours are also available. Thick cardstock is usually used as the base to avoid buckling.

There are various forms of triple embossing. An image can be stamped and coloured before layers of clear UTEE are applied over the top. This gives the impression of looking through enamel to the design underneath. UTEE can also be applied to a thinner cardstock and, once dry, placed into the refridgerator for a few minutes to fully harden before being gently bent so that the enamel cracks. This is known as 'shattered glass'.

This project uses the method of colouring thick card before adding several layers of UTEE and then stamping directly into the molten enamel. Wooden backed rubber stamps are the most suitable for this project as they're unaffected by being pressed into the hot surface.

Mount card (as used in picture framing) is a perfect weight to use, but card from packaging, such as the backing in new shirts, is a good alternative. If the card is too thin it will buckle as the second layer of UTEE is heated and the liquid enamel will tend to run down the sides leaving a thinner area in the centre.

As the liquid UTEE gets very hot, it's advisable to use a wooden kebab skewer to manouevre the card. Placing the panel onto a piece of thin card is a good way to hold it for heating and allows the heat to pass through, which melts the powder more quickly.

When the final layer of UTEE has been added you need to have everything ready for the next stage. So, ink up the stamp and have the lids off any jars of embossing powder or glitter so they're easily accessible. Heat the final layer of powder and sprinkle any extra colours onto the surface before pressing the stamp firmly into the panel. Hold in place for a few seconds and then allow the enamel to cool down for about 30 seconds before gently removing the stamp.

Once you've tried this technique, do experiment with various stamps, inks etc and have fun seeing what effects can be achieved. The beauty is that no two pieces will come out the same and there's always an element of anticipation!

Step by Step Instructions

You will need:

- Rubber stamp: Windswept Girl P1544D by Personal Impressions
- Ultra Thick Embossing Enamel (UTEE) clear
- Embossing powders in gold and white
- Versamagic Dewdrop inkpads in Wheat, Sahara Sand and Jumbo Java
- Piece of thick card (mountcard is ideal)
- Brown and gold card stock
- Decorative vellum
- Three brown silk flowers, including one beaded one
- 2 x medium gold brads
- 15cm square cream card blank
- Metallic gold pen
- Clear embossing inkpad

Hints & Tips Try adding glitter, gold leaf or Mica powders to the final layer of melted UTEE. Don't add micro beads as these will damage the stamp when it's pressed down onto them.

Cut a piece of thick card to approx 5.5cm square and apply the three Versamagic inks, from light to dark, directly to the surface.

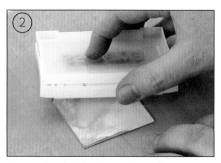

Once the ink is dry rub a clear embossing inkpad over the surface.

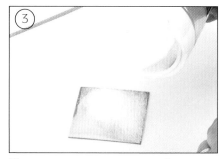

Place the panel onto a piece of thin card and hold in the air whilst applying heat until melted.

Place onto scrap paper and pour the UTEE over then tip off the excess.

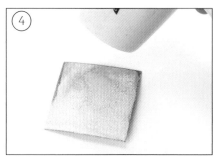

Immediately pour a second layer of UTEE over the melted surface. Tip off excess.

Heat and add a third layer of the UTEE but do not heat yet.

Remove the lids from the gold and white embossing powders. Ink up the stamp with the Jumb Java inkpad.

Now heat the panel again, noting that it may take slightly longer to melt having been allowed to cool slightly.

Sprinkle gold and white powders onto the surface and apply a little more heat.

Immediately press stamp into surface, allow to cool and then lift away – you may need to peel card back from the stamp.

Edge panel with gold pen and stick onto gold and then brown card, trimming narrow borders on each. Use double-sided tape to ensure good adhesion.

Cut a piece of decorative vellum to 13.5cm square and a piece of brown card to 13cm square. Hold the vellum over the brown card.

Place two brown flowers onto left and bottom of vellum and pierce holes through centres and both layers before attaching them with gold brads.

Stick the square to the centre of the card blank and add a third, beaded flower below the first two using a glue dot or silicone glue.

Add a little tape between the vellum and brown card at the top right and then stick the stamped panel to the vellum over this.

Distressing a stamped image

Sometimes a stamped image can be enhanced by knocking back the colour somewhat, such as with a vintage, antiquarian or oriental theme. This technique can be helpful for anyone who is not confident with their colouring abilities too, as any irregularities in the shading can be disguised by the blending of the inks.

There are various ways of blending the inks on the card surface, though results will vary with each. Cheap, man-made sponge can be used and will give a more textural, less blended finish. Finer sponges, such as cosmetic types, will blend better than the rougher types. Cut n Dry Foam is made with ink blending in mind and comes in sheets which can be cut into small pieces when needed. It has a foam surface and a rubbery backing which allows it to be held and gives it stability. There's also the option of buying ready-cut pieces of foam with a fuzzy backing which grips onto a Velcro surface on an applicator tool.

Distress inkpads are perfect for this effect as they're designed to blend smoothly together without streaky marks. They can be used by picking up the ink with the foam, or the pads can be pressed onto a craft sheet (or non-stick surface) and then the ink used from here.

The card that is being distressed should be held flat to the craft sheet with the fingers of one hand whilst the foam should be held in the other. Move the foam in a circular motion, picking up a little ink and then lightly blend onto the card, still using a circular action. The card should be turned slowly with the fingers so that the edges are inked all round. A second shade of ink can now be applied in the same way so that the two colours blend together. All the Distress ink colours work well together, so any combination will give a good effect.

Sanding the edge of the inked piece is an option which will enhance the antique, distressed look. You can use either a dedicated distressing edger, a piece of sandpaper or even an emery board. Simply run your chosen tool down the edges of the card to roughen them up and then blend a darker shade of ink along the ragged surface.

Step by Step Instructions

- Rubber stamps:
  Fire Dragon P1397N
  by Personal Impressions
  Music and Joy P1392C
  by Personal Impressions
- Black Archival (or other permanent) inkpad
- Distress inkpads in Old Paper, Vintage Photo and Walnut Stain
- Cut n Dry foam
- Cream card on which to stamp
- Black and red card stock
- Distressing tool or sandpaper
- Sheer red ribbon – approximately 3/4 metre
- 6 x black, self-adhesive gem stones
- Cream DL card blank
- Brush pens in yellow, orange, red and green

Stamp the dragon onto a 6cm x 11cm panel of cream card using the black Archival inkpad.

Colour along the edge of the dragon with a yellow brush pen and fill in the horns. Colour the tongue in red.

Use an orange pen along the centre of the dragon's body, face and ears. Don't worry about colouring neatly!

Colour the eye in green and add red to the remaining areas. The dragon should be filled in but if there are any uncoloured areas showing, this is fine.

Hints & Tips
When distressing the card blank itself, place a piece of scrap paper inside it to stop it catching any ink.

Use light shades over the largest area of the panel and darker shades nearest to the edges to give a smooth graduation of colour.

Press ink from Old Paper inkpad onto craft sheet. Pick up colour with foam and use circular motion to blend ink around edges of card and bring a little colour over image as well.

Repeat step five using the Vintage Photo ink, working lightly so as not to make the colour too heavy.

Roughen the edges with sandpaper or a distressing tool.

Use the Walnut Stain ink as before to darken the roughened edges.

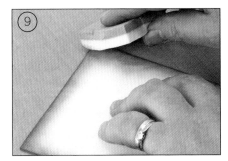

Repeat the distressing process directly onto the front of the card, just around the edges.

Mat the dragon image onto black and then red card, trimming small borders all round. Adhere to the front of the card towards the top.

Stamp the Music and Joy image onto red card using black ink. Cut into a square, mat onto black card and stick below dragon using 3D foam.

Wrap the ribbon around the spine of the card and tie at the top, trimming the ends into points.

Stick three self-adhesive black gemstones to each end of the ribbon.

Shrink plastic bag charm

Shrink plastic is a fascinating material that can be used to create miniature versions of any stamp to add to cards, jewellery etc. Because the images not only shrink to around seven times their original size but also become thicker, they are quite strong and therefore ideal for the bag charm in this project.

Shrink plastic is available in several types and is usually sold in packs of sheets that can be stamped, coloured and cut out. Clear, black, white, coloured and frosted are all popular, but I recommend the frosted for beginners to start with as it has a rough side which is easier to stamp and colour than the other finishes. Stamping is best done with a permanent inkpad, such as Stazon, as this will not smudge and it gives a crisp image with no bleeding of the lines as may happen with oil-based inks for instance.

When colouring the design remember that, as the plastic shrinks, the colours will intensify and deepen, so always choose paler shades than you wish the finished image to be. Pencil crayons, Marvy Le Plume pens and gel pens are all good choices for this surface. Here I have used glitter gel pens with a paintbrush to soften the depth of colour. The glitter effect also becomes stronger, so these are the perfect choice to use with the fairy stamps.

All cutting out and punching of holes must be done before shrinking as the plastic will be too thick afterwards. Holes will shrink too of course, so a standard office punch is perfect to make the correctly sized loop for a jump ring or thread.

The plastic can be heated in the oven when placed onto a tray lined with Teflon or tin foil – read individual manufacturer's instructions for specific temperatures. However, most people prefer to use a heat tool: the 'hairdryer' types, which are slightly gentler than other models, are the most suitable. A wooden kebab skewer is ideal for manouevring the piece as you heat it as it will not stick to the plastic.

Apply heat to the image, keeping the skewer hovering above to prevent it from blowing away, and, as it starts to shrink and curl, flip it over, as it is vital to heat the back as well to prevent distortion. Flip it back over again and continue to heat until the image stops shrinking and then immediately press a heavy smooth object on top of it to keep it flat (the back of a wooden stamp is ideal for this). Allow the piece to cool before using.

Step by Step Instructions

Ink up each of the fairies with the Stazon pad and stamp them onto the rough side of the shrink plastic.

You will need:

- Frosted shrink plastic
- Stamps:
  Elegant Fairy JS39M and
  Fairy on Branch JS24Q
  both Joanna Sheen
  from Personal Impressions
  Fairy P735G and P736G
  both by Personal Impressions
  Live, Laugh, Love 5009e
  Inca Stamp
- Sakura Stardust gel pens in
  clear and assorted shades
- Bag charm clasp – silver
- 6mm jump rings – silver
- Eyepins – silver
- Sheer ribbon
- Rocaille beads in pink, blue
  and lilac
- 6mm crystal beads
- Wooden kebab skewer
- Non-stick craft sheet
- Jewellery pliers
- 5mm hole punch
- Stazon inkpad, black

Take orange glitter gel pen, touch it to a fairy face, just on hairline, and use waterbrush to soften colour and paint face and neck.

Colour the rest of the fairy image in the same way, adding the pen colours onto the black lines and then brushing the colours out to soften.

Once dry, punch hole just above head. Carefully cut around image using fine-pointed scissors, leaving a very small border all around fairy and hole.

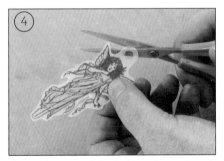

Place fairy onto the non-stick sheet and hold skewer just above it to prevent it moving. Use heat tool to start the shrinking process.

Once the plastic has begun to shrink and curl, flip it over and heat the back.

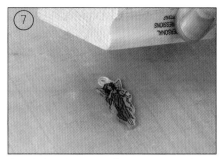

Flip it back to the front to complete the shrinking and then place a flat object on top of it. Repeat the colouring and shrinking with each fairy.

Stamp message onto shrink plastic and go over words with clear glitter gel pen. Add a few simple stars around words with coloured glitter pens.

Cut into a panel and punch a hole in one corner before shrinking as before. Edge the shrunken panel with a silver pen.

Open jump ring and thread it through one of the fairies, using small pliers to close it. Add more rings and then attach to bag charm clasp.

Thread a crystal bead onto an eyepin, followed by a few rocaille beads.

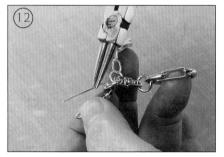

Bend the end of the eyepin round, latch onto the clasp and squeeze shut with the pliers, trimming off any excess wire.

Attach all the fairies and message to the clasp or eyepins.

Tie length of sheer ribbon to clasp with double knot. Trim ends to points and thread crystal bead onto each one before knotting ends and trimming. Repeat with second ribbon.

Working with Stampbord

Stampbord is a wonderful, clay-based product to use rubber stamps on, as it's incredibly smooth and white, so it picks up every detail easily. Inks can be sponged or rolled onto the surface to give a coloured background and the surface can be scratched into to reveal the white clay beneath. It has a hard backing so it does not bend or cockle even when heated or saturated with ink.

Any inkpads can be used to colour the Stampbord surface. Apply the lightest colour first and build up the colour in stages, applying even pressure for a smooth blend. Once dry, the surface can then be stamped onto, and/or scratched into with a scraping tool – though you can use a fine craft knife as a good alternative to start with. Do ensure that the ink colours are dry before scraping though as, if they're wet, the tool will dig in too much and gouge the clay, as opposed to finely scratching it. If you decide to go further with this lovely medium then it's worth investing in a range of different tools to etch the surface.

The sky effect in this project was easily achieved on the ultra smooth surface and the stars and the details on the branches and owl were lightly scratched in afterwards.

Because of its hard quality, Stampbord can also be made into jewellery such as brooches and pendants. A brooch back can be adhered with Glossy Accents for a strong bond, or the piece can be drilled to attach a jump ring or bale to accept a chain or cord. The Cropodile tool will also punch through Stampbord with no problem.

You will need:

- Stampbord large oval
- Rubber stamps:
  Fluffy Owl FH116
  Reach for the Moon FN74
  both by Funstamps
- Versamagic Dewdrop inkpads in Aspen Mist, Aegean Blue and Night Sky
- Black Stazon inkpad
- Brush pens in black, yellow, light brown and beige
- Scraper tool or fine bladed craft knife
- Silver marker pen
- Glossy Accents
- Silver, black and white card
- 4cm circle punch
- White DL card blank
- Ultra-strong double-sided tape

Reach for the moon, if you don't make it you'll still be amongst the stars!

Step by Step Instructions

Lightly dab the sponge onto the Aspen Mist inkpad then sweep it across the Stampbord surface using even pressure.

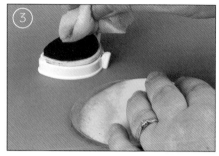

Pick up Aegean Blue on a different side of the sponge and sweep this over the surface, blending into the light blue.

Repeat with Night Sky, concentrating most of the colour around the top and right side of the oval. Blend well with the sponge.

Ink up the Fluffy Owl stamp with the black Stazon pad and press firmly onto the centre of the oval.

With the black pen, draw a simple branch from left to right making sure to fill in between the owl's feet so he appears to be perching.

Use the brush pens to colour the owl, using one shade for the face and tummy, one for the head, wings and tail, and another for the beak and feet.

Hints & Tips You can sweep a clear pigment inkpad across the surface and add two coats of clear embossing powder to give an enamelled surface which is ideal if you're creating a jewellery piece.

Because the Stampbord is quite heavy, trim the bottom edge of the back of the card at a shallow angle so that the card tips back slightly. This will ensure that the card does not fall over when displayed.

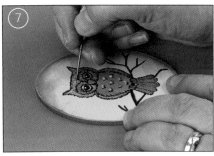

Once colours are fully dry, take scraper tool, or fine craft knife, and gently scratch fine lines onto owl's plumage. This adds texture and lightens colour.

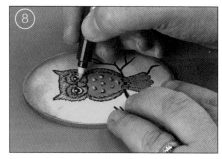

Scratch the eye details to emphasise the white and then use a yellow pen to colour the irises.

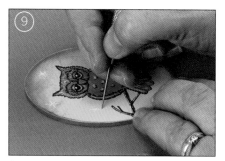

Scrape white lines along the top edges of the branch and scratch simple star shapes into the background.

Use silver pen to edge around sides of the oval. Mat a 8.5cm x 19cm piece of white card onto black card, trimming a border all round. Stick to card blank.

Ink up word stamp with Night Sky and stamp onto white card. Cut into a panel, mat onto black and silver card and stick to bottom of card using 3D foam.

Use ultra-strong tape to attach the owl panel to the top of the card and draw simple silver stars around it.

Punch circle of silver card, place it halfway back in and punch again to create crescent. Secure to top right of card with three layers of 3D foam.

Add drops of Glossy Accents to the eyes, beak and feet to highlight them.

Stamping on acetate

Acetate is a wonderful and versatile material to work with and whereas it was once difficult to find products that would work with its ultra smooth surface, now there are many inks and pens which are perfectly suited to it.

As well as ordinary acetate, a heat embossable version is also widely available and this is the type used here. This will not melt nor buckle when used with a heat tool, though care should always be taken not to over-heat it.

This project makes full use of the acetate's transparency to create a candle shade which will cast a colourful glow once placed over a small candle or tealight inside a glass jar. If being sent as a gift, it can be posted flat and then simply formed into the cylinder shape and secured with the high-tack tape along the edge.

Alcohol inks are used to create the background colour as these are also transparent thereby allowing the light to glow through. These inks are invaluable as they will work on tricky glossy surfaces such as glass, metal, plastic, foil, gloss card and, of course, acetate.

There are various options for which type of ink can be used for the black silhouette images. Stazon can be used if stamped onto the reverse of the acetate, ie: not on top of the alcohol inks, as, being a solvent-based ink, it will remove the colour. A black pigment ink can also be used with clear embossing powder, but, as this is a candle shade, it is best to avoid this method as the embossed images could be affected by the heat. Adirondack pigment ink in Pitch Black is the perfect solution as it can be heat set on acetate.

You will need:

- A4 sheet of heat embossable acetate
- Alcohol inks in Stream, Wild Plum and Stonewashed (or your choice)
- Alcohol blending solution
- Alcohol ink applicator tool with felt
- Adirondack Pigment inkpad in Pitch Black
- Fairy silhouette stamp (I used 'Flying Fairy' by Arts Encaustic)
- Wild Flowers silhouette stamp (I used Hero Arts Design Block S5033)
- Iridescent glitter glue such as Stickles Diamond
- Heat tool
- Ultra-strong double-sided tape
- Pricking tool or large needle
- Spongy surface, such as an old mouse mat

Step by Step Instructions

① Press a felt piece onto the wooden applicator tool and make sure that it's held firmly in place.

② Apply the nozzle of the Stream alcohol ink against the felt and squeeze gently for a couple of seconds – you'll see the ink spread out slightly.

Hints & Tips When using the alcohol inks, bring the bottle and the tool towards each other, rather than tipping the nozzle onto the felt. This will stop the ink from spurting out where you don't want it. Use other colours of the alcohol inks to create various background effects, remembering that the colours will look lighter when the light shines through.

③ Repeat with the Wild Plum and the Stonewashed colours, being sure to add them in different areas of the felt.

④ Squeeze a few drops of the alcohol blending solution onto the felt.

⑤ Stamp the applicator tool all over the acetate sheet, turning it in your hand as you do so.

Hints & Tips Only add tiny amounts of glitter glue as if you apply heavy dots they will not stick well to the acetate.

For a last-minute gift, create the background and use black rub-ons to decorate the acetate.

Add a little more ink to tool, a little extra blending solution and repeat step five. This will make colours blend together. Allow to dry which should take less than a minute.

Turn acetate sheet over. Ink up the wild flowers stamp with Pitch Black ink, position at bottom of one long edge and press down firmly all over to ensure a good image.

Gently heat set the ink with the heat tool – you'll see it turn from glossy to a matt finish as it dries.

Repeat across the edge of the acetate. Now ink up the fairy and stamp onto the area above the flowers. Heat to set and then repeat twice more.

Place the acetate onto a spongy surface and use a pricking tool, or large needle, to poke several holes randomly into the background.

Add tiny dots of glitter glue to some of the flower heads and around the pricked holes to look like star shapes. Allow to set.

Apply a strip of ultra-strong double-sided tape down one narrow edge of the acetate.

To use the shade, remove backing from tape, form acetate into a tube and stick edge down. Put a tealight candle into a glass jar and place shade over it.

IMPORTANT:
Never place a candle directly within the acetate shade. Always use it inside a glass jar and place the acetate tube over this. Never leave a burning candle unattended.

Masking a stamped image

A great way to make your stamps even more versatile is to use the masking technique. This allows you to build up a scene from several stamps, or create an extended image from one stamp as in this project. Here, a group of four cats is turned into a full-blown choir!

The secret tool behind masking is the humble Post-it note. These paper sheets, with a low-tack adhesive strip, can be adhered to the stamped card and then removed again without damaging the image or card surface. It's possible to use plain paper, but there's always the chance that this would move, which would cause problems.

Masking is a simple technique once the basic premise is grasped, and you may find yourself looking at your stamp collection to find images that will lend themselves to it. The main thing to remember is that the image which is stamped first will appear to be further forward than those stamped over it.

The image should be stamped onto a Post-it note, making sure that the adhesive strip on the reverse is incorporated within it. Once cut out, this will be a self-adhesive mask. Make sure that you cut the mask accurately, slightly inside the outline, as this will prevent a halo of white between the stamped images.

Stamp the same image onto card and then place the mask directly on top of it, making sure that everything lines up. Now stamp a second image so that part of it is on top of the first, masked one. Once you remove the Post-it note you'll see that the second image appears to be behind the first one. You can decide how many images to add, simply moving the mask from one section to another before stamping again.

You can choose to use one stamp, as in this project, or several different ones. For instance, you may have several snowmen stamps and, rather than lining them up, or cutting them out and layering them over each other, masking allows you to form them into a group directly onto the card. Cottages, trees and other rural images can all be masked to create a unique landscape.

You will need:

- Rubber stamp: Cat's Choir FM183 by Funstamps
- Black dye-based inkpad
- Coloured pencils
- Post-it notes
- Navy blue felt tipped pen
- White DL card blank
- Thin white card
- Thin navy blue card or paper
- Paw print punch

Step by Step Instructions

Example of a
landscape created
from several stamps.

Stamp the cats onto a Post-it note,
checking that the adhesive strip is
included within the image.

Carefully cut out the image, being
sure to cut slightly within the
outline.

Stamp the cats into the centre of a
piece of white card.

Place the mask directly on top of
the stamped cats, lining it up
accurately.

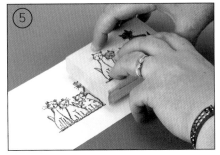

Stamp the cats onto the card again so
that the image is partly covering the
Post-it note and partly to the right of
it. Make sure to line up the feet.

You will see that the second group
of cats is now partly behind the first
group.

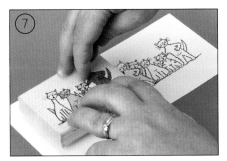

Replace mask and stamp the cats again, this time on top of and slightly to the left of the first, masked one.

Remove the mask to reveal the line of cats, some behind and some in front.

Colour the cats, being sure to make them all look quite different as this helps with the illusion. Add some green below the feet to anchor the cats to the ground.

Trim image to 7cm x 20.5cm and mat onto piece of navy blue card. Stick strip of white card to the reverse so that a few mm show below bottom edge.

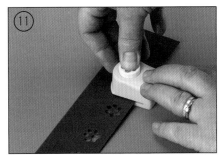

Cut a 4cm strip of navy card and punch a line of paw prints along it. Trim the strip to the same length as the cat image.

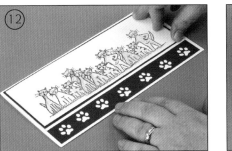

Stick the paw print strip across the bottom of the card front and the cat panel above it so that it overlaps.

Use a navy blue pen to write 'Have a purrfect birthday!' in one corner, using stick and dot writing. Draw on simple musical notes.

Hints & Tips Buy the largest size of Post-It notes that you can, as you will be able to use these with bigger stamps.

When colouring animals with crayons allow the pencil strokes to show, as this will give texture to the fur.

When I count my blessings
I always count you twice

Using fantasy fibres

For a shimmery sparkle, fantasy fibres are hard to beat. They are strands of fusible fibre which come in tightly packed bundles ready to be teased out in whatever amount you wish to use. There are lots of colours available, from garish pinks, through dark blues to transparent, iridescent shades. The fibres can be fused together by ironing them, or they can be used as they are to add a twinkling accent.

As well as fibres, fantasy film can also be purchased. This usually comes in packs containing long rolled up strips. The film can be layered or cut up before fusing, and can also be combined with the fibres to create interesting effects. Both are very economical to use, in that there is absolutely no waste – every scrap can be used.

The fibres can be ironed between two layers of greaseproof paper (or vellum) to create sheets of handmade 'paper', or they can be used in conjunction with rubber stamps.

Wooden backed, rubber stamps are the best choice here, as they are unaffected by the heat, and the wood gives stability whilst ironing. A dry iron must always be used, so, if you don't have a dedicated craft iron, remember to turn off the steam, or empty the water from, your normal iron.

The stamp must be inked and then fibres, or film, are placed on top, covered with paper and then ironed. When ironing, press down and hold, rather than using a normal smoothing movement. The image will show through the greaseproof paper once it is ready. Try mixing various colours of fibres, or combining fibres and film, and see what various effects you can achieve.

They are a perfect way of giving a gossamer look to a dragonfly, or butterfly image, or, as here, the stamped image can be highlighted with colour from a brush pen for a slighlty different effect.

You will need:

- Fantasy fibre, yellow
- Rubber stamps:
  Patchwork Flower FP110
  by Funstamps
  Sentiment from 'Count my Blessings' set PICS012
  by Personal Impressions
- Brush pens in orange, pink and green
- Permanent black inkpad
- Green dye-based inkpad
- Cardstock in green, yellow and white
- Sheer green ribbon
- 6in x 8in / 15cm x 20.5cm white card blank – I cut mine from A3 white card so I could have the spine on the short edge, but you could use a bought card with the fold at the top.
- Iron (set to no steam)
- Greaseproof paper or vellum

Step by Step Instructions

Ink up the stamp with permanent black ink and lay it, on its back, on your worksurface.

Tease out a handful of the fibres and lay them over the stamp, ensuring that the whole image is covered.

Place a sheet of greaseproof paper (or vellum) on top of the fibres.

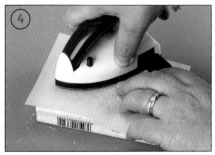

WIth the iron set to medium, press down over the stamp and hold in place for around three seconds – you'll see the image coming through the paper.

Lift off the iron and peel the paper away before removing the fibres from the stamp.

Tease away any excess fibres from the image, though you may wish to leave an edge around it.

Use the brush pens to lightly colour chosen areas of the image. Stick the image to a 7cm x 11cm piece of white card. Mat onto green, and then white card, trimming narrow borders all round.

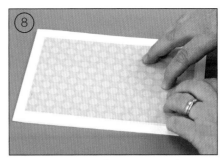

Mat a 12cm x 18cm piece of decorative green paper onto yellow card, trim a narrow border and stick onto the card front.

Mat a 5cm wide strip of yellow card onto white, trim a border and cut to 18cm in length. Stick across the card near the bottom.

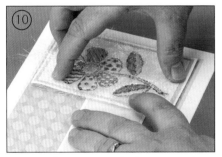

Use 3D foam to stick the matted image to the right of the card.

Use the green ink to stamp the sentiment onto white card. Trim into a panel and mat onto green and white card.

Tease out a small amount of the fantasy fibres and stick onto the yellow strip with double-sided tape.

Stick the message panel over the fibres using 3D foam.

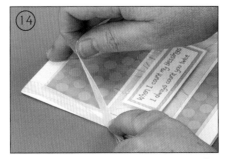

Tie the ribbon around the spine of the card.

Hints & Tips

When using the film, try trapping metallic glitter between a couple of sheets for an extra sparkle.

The fused fibres, or film, can be cut into shapes, so you can use them to create wings, petals etc for three dimensional projects such as Christmas decorations.

Candle stamping

Inexpensive, plain candles can be decorated very easily with stamped images to make gifts or to match the decor in your home. Although it's possible to stamp directly onto the candle, it's much easier, and more versatile, to stamp onto tissue and then apply the image to the surface.

Round candles, for instance, are tricky to work directly onto as a wooden stamp would have to be rolled across the surface, or a clear, or unmounted stamp, 'cupped' in the hand.

This technique works best on cheaper candles as they tend to melt more quickly. It's also worth buying the type that burn down in the centre whilst leaving a wall of wax intact, as, once burned part way down, a tealight can be placed inside the cavity and the light will glow from within to illuminate the stamped image. Work with thick candles for the best effect.

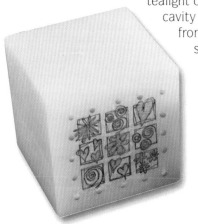

Any stamps can be used to suit your style and they can be left monochrome or coloured with your preferred medium.

Stamp onto the dull side of white tissue paper and colour in with your chosen pens or pencils and then cut out the image, leaving a small border all round. Slightly dampen the back of the tissue and position it on the candle – the dampness helps the paper to stay in place. Smooth it down and wrap the candle in greaseproof paper.

Switch on the heat tool and allow it to get warmed up for a few seconds before aiming it at the candle and keeping it moving slowly across the surface. You'll see the greaseproof paper becoming translucent as the surface wax melts. Once the stamped image is visible switch off the heat tool and remove the greaseproof paper. The stamped tissue will now be embedded below a thin layer of wax.

The wax will stay malleable for long enough to push decorative items into the surface to further embellish it if you wish. Brads, eyelets or glass beads, threaded onto short pins, are all suitable.

Step by Step Instructions

Stamp the image onto the dull side of white tissue paper using a black inkpad.

Colour the image in. (I used glitter gel pens applied directly for a lovely sparkle.)

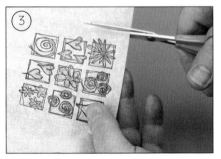

Cut the tissue paper out so that there is a small border all round the image.

Dampen the back of the tissue paper with a light spritz of water.

Position the tissue onto the candle and press into place.

Wrap a piece of greaseproof paper around the candle and hold it tightly against the surface.

Warm up the heat tool and aim it at the candle, keeping it moving to avoid over-heating one area. You'll see the greaseproof paper becoming translucent and the image beginning to appear.

Hints & Tips If you're working with a round candle, wrap greaseproof paper around the front and hold the ends tightly at the back so that it is smooth and pressed against the surface whilst it is being heated. This keeps the candle surface smooth and stops it from dripping.

Choose reasonably strong colours for your stamped images as they will be slightly toned down when they have a thin layer of wax over them.

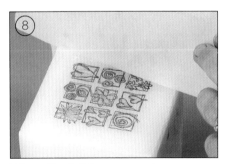

When the full image can be seen, carefully remove the greaseproof paper.

Push in small matching brads around the stamped image.

Index